MAY
DAY

BOOKS BY PHILLIS LEVIN

POETRY

Temples and Fields
The Afterimage
Mercury
May Day

ANTHOLOGY

The Penguin Book of the Sonnet:
500 Years of a Classic Tradition in English

MAY DAY

Phillis
Levin

PENGUIN POETS

PENGUIN BOOKS
Published by the Penguin Group
Penguin Group (USA) Inc., 375 Hudson Street, New York, New York 10014, U.S.A.
Penguin Group (Canada), 90 Eglinton Avenue East, Suite 700, Toronto, Ontario,
Canada M4P 2Y3 (a division of Pearson Penguin Canada Inc.)
Penguin Books Ltd, 80 Strand, London WC2R 0RL, England
Penguin Ireland, 25 St Stephen's Green, Dublin 2, Ireland (a division of Penguin Books Ltd)
Penguin Group (Australia), 250 Camberwell Road, Camberwell, Victoria 3124, Australia
(a division of Pearson Australia Group Pty Ltd)
Penguin Books India Pvt Ltd, 11 Community Centre, Panchsheel Park,
New Delhi – 110 017, India
Penguin Group (NZ), 67 Apollo Drive, Rosedale, North Shore 0632, New Zealand
(a division of Pearson New Zealand Ltd)
Penguin Books (South Africa) (Pty) Ltd, 24 Sturdee Avenue, Rosebank,
Johannesburg 2196, South Africa

Penguin Books Ltd, Registered Offices:
80 Strand, London WC2R 0RL, England

First published in Penguin Books 2008

1   3   5   7   9   10   8   6   4   2

Pages 73–74 constitute an extension of this copyright page.

LIBRARY OF CONGRESS CATALOGING IN PUBLICATION DATA
Levin, Phillis, 1954–
May day / Phillis Levin.
p.   cm.
ISBN 978-0-14-311394-2
I. Title.
PS3562.E88966M39 2008
811'.54—dc22 2008003860

Printed in the United States of America
Set in Janson MT with Van Dijck MT ·   · Designed by Sabrina Bowers

For JSS

Now and always

CONTENTS

As Reason is a Rebel unto Faith, so Passion unto Reason: As the propositions of Faith seem absurd unto Reason, so the Theorems of Reason unto Passion, and both unto Faith.

SIR THOMAS BROWNE, *Religio Medici*

MAY
DAY

MAY DAY

I've decided to waste my life again,
Like I used to: get drunk on
The light in the leaves, find a wall
Against which something can happen,

Whatever may have happened
Long ago—let a bullet hole echoing
The will of an executioner, a crevice
In which a love note was hidden,

Be a cell where a struggling tendril
Utters a few spare syllables at dawn.
I've decided to waste my life
In a new way, to forget whoever

Touched a hair on my head, because
It doesn't matter what came to pass,
Only that it passed, because we repeat
Ourselves, we repeat ourselves.

I've decided to walk a long way
Out of the way, to allow something
Dreaded to waken for no good reason,
Let it go without saying,

Let it go as it will to the place
It will go without saying: a wall
Against which a body was pressed
For no good reason, other than this.

A NEEDLE IN THE SKY

There is a needle in the sky
    Being threaded now, but the thread is blue:
That is why you cannot see it
    Threading its way. When all is said and done
It will keep sewing—as long
    As a tiny knot remains, as long as something
Whets the tip whenever the knot
    Happens to untie, as long as the sun
Arouses the wind that catches
    The thread again, twisting an end so that
It may begin. There is a needle
    Pulling a thread through your veins,
A needle pulling the sap
    From the root to the bole, a thread
Pulling a bird to a tree—
    Tugging your heart as soon as you believe
There is nothing left.
    There is a glistening filament, a cold
Instrument making its way
    From once upon a time to now,
To tomorrow. Maybe the sun
    Is a giant spool, maybe the needle
Cannot rest until it runs
    Out of light, maybe a star is a random
Stitch unraveling...
    Until a needle runs out of thread,
It is impossible to look
    Into its eye.

ACORN

Under its hat
many secrets
asleep
keeping time

Soon it will tell
almost everything

if you wait
long enough
in the grass in the snow

if you look if you listen

and if you do nothing
it will be what it will be
nevertheless

With a hat like that
you could walk the windiest hall
of an endless wood

as the worst and the best rain down
out of nowhere

With a hat like that
you could hide the highest hope
the biggest fear

and appear once a year to disappear

O where is the loom
on which it is woven

How can a tomb
too small for a petal
carry the body of autumn in its hull

Cradle of greenest memory

kernel dreaming
the weight of a starling

cupola cupping the fire of dawn

den of creation
shedding itself
again
for a song

O give me a room to keep a secret
until the leaf is ready
to be lit

and when it is time to go out
into the cold
give me a hat
like that

BORN FOR THE SNOW

We were born to be blessed, to be torn into being
Alive, to be weary and open and lost,
Carrying ourselves

As the weight of the planet spins us into light.
We were born to say this, beholding,
Beholden to everything here

Before and after fire and water,
Earth and air. We were born for the snow
To fall on us over and over,

Anonymous leaflets
Glimmering far and near, arriving
Without being read, seraphs

Of unrecounted history
Sending an inaudible reply.
We were born for the birth to be borne

To the end of time, to know
It is time, no matter the time, though today
Everything is as it is

Without anything in the world
Covering the door
To things as they are:

Confetti of laughter rising
From a town, a festival
Dying down, floating by,

A field being fed by the snow.

IN PRAISE OF PARTICLES

jot
tittle
dot

modicum
minim
whit

scintilla
cinder
bit

snippet
jab
mite

splinter
pip
scrap

archaeon
micron
crumb

dram
dash
snap

shred
fleck
flake

stipple
freckle
speckle

dapple
dab
blot

splotch
mote
spot

morsel
smidgeon
grain

INCHWORM

Inchworm finding a path
To heaven, climbing a cable
That from a leaf dangles,

Only you, fizz of a green star,
Wander from where to where
Without fear. Because the line

Was too low we could not
See it, because it was too fine
We did not feel it, so we fell,

Without knowing why. The tree
Of knowledge & the tree of life
Are intertwined, struggling

Together to ascend: they will
Strangle each other or bend,
And their ascent may end

In their undoing. Inchworm
Hugging a slender trail,
Scaling a sliver of time

From which we dangle,
Are you the true measure
Stretching across the divide?

VIEW FROM A TERRACE IN ANTIBES

Homage to Nicolas de Staël

Let me draw an analogy:

I want to jump into it,
to be inside
what I see,

as if light alone
could be a door.

But the analogy fails,

I cannot name
what calls me
to this lush landscape,

the double windows
in your tower

opening onto
the gulf across the ramparts.

*

Loss after loss peels away,
exposing

thickets of sublimity,
an incandescent wound,
bounty unbound.

It will be the scene
of your final action,

whatever else you finish
or leave undone.

*

The fierce drive to enter the body of the world,
not to take anything but to render it,
to adore and endure the beloved,

is to make another thing entirely,

using oneself
entirely
until what is within becomes so real

anyone seeing it
can enter in.

So I want to plunge my being
without harm to myself or another
into the landscape you have made.

*

Is there escape in landscape
if it arouses every memory,

unveiling every face?

*

When you knew
she would never return to you

did a pale figure appear
across the gulf,

inviting you to leap,
to join a shadow in the air

above the stark ramparts,

their stony fingers unable to catch
anything
but light?

*

Sometimes I walk along a cliff of color,
over one edge onto another,

there is always more:

a plenitude feeding the eye
like a well giving all that it promises
without ending in metaphor.

*

A brush and a knife

met a palette
of noise and silence

on a day
not long ago
in a room in a town by the sea.

LETTER TO THE SNOW

Why aren't you here?

I await your arrival.

It is better when you surround me.

Why does it matter at all
that you haven't arrived, if I know
you will appear one day sooner or later?

It would be better for it to be sooner.

If I know you are there, outside
or about to be,
it is easy to breathe freely,

to arise and sleep being held by your light.

This morning a flower on the sill opened
and opened, and the sound
of its opening was the sound of your landing.

TENDER OFFER

for Jean Valentine

That little chick on the sidewalk
on the pink
stone steps
whose gravel glistened

That little boy who brought it by
brought it to me
in the cup
of his hands

where he held it
untrembling

A living thing
butter-yellow ashes

a living thing

Tiny body
(some body's) being
felt

softer than   soft as

the collection of all erasures

Butter-yellow ash heap / featherbed
breathing inside his hands

dandelion pillow with two puny legs
twig feet

One little body giving light
a cup of light
of tenderness   waking

So much work already done

MY BROTHER'S SHIRT

I ask my brother
Did he put on his shirt
To go through the long passage

Where is the shirt for that journey
Shirt of love
Shirt of blood

*

I ask my brother
Did he take off his shirt
To go through the long passage

Where is the shirt for that journey
Shirt of blood
Shirt of love

THAT MORNING

A woman leaned against a wall, sobbing
"The people, the people." A broken urn

lay on its side, the soil spilling out,
the roots of the plant exposed,

though its form remained intact.
There was a birch a block away

that I fled to—a shoal of light shivering
in its leaves, a scroll peeling from its skin.

I returned to the street where I lived
to see a man sitting down on his briefcase:

he was staring out at something—
I couldn't speak to him,

a gulf opened between us
as he peered into the distance,

into the air. I could taste the future,
a taste of impossible things.

Then I went into Antonio's café:
his mother made coffee for everyone,

refusing to take any money
(she was waiting for a call from her son).

A man with a big portfolio stepped in,
walking over to the bar where we sat.

We waited together,
looking down at the marble,

looking up at a television screen,
though what we saw

was happening outside.
We needed to be near each other,

under the circumstances.
The man with the big portfolio

pointed to the screen and said,
"This means war"—his declaration

harboring a wild cold joy,
his jaw an engine of resolve.

Some of us put two
and two together:

hadn't there been a storm
the night before?

Rain, so much rain,
gushing from gutters,

flooding our shoes.
Isn't that why the urn

overturned, isn't that why
there wasn't a cloud in the sky?

One by one we left, going
our separate ways into the air

that for many weeks
was not the air we knew.

THE CHARIOT

I was sitting in bed, thinking of the rage of Achilles.
He had been on my mind for a while. I was going
Over the lines, occupying the space in which

He knows it is time to surrender the body of Hector,
But does not know Priam will enter his tent,
Empty-handed Priam begging for the corpse of his son,

When an image arose of a coffee shop called The Chariot,
A landmark that suddenly disappeared. One day
It just wasn't there, though as far back

As anyone remembers it was filled with customers
Pouring out of the subway at 14th Street and the Avenue
Of the Americas, heading a block south to the Village,

Hungry for something cheap and substantial,
Too much in a hurry to go any farther; or someone
Like myself, who lived nearby. It was a decent place,

Well lit, too brightly lit—a retinue of waiters
(Never a woman among them) carrying platters
As generous as those voluminous menus, shouting

Commands across the aisles: *Whiskey down.*
Over light. A smear. A civilized place, a place
To take the kids or be alone, to read the paper

Or think about things. A boy on every placemat
Played his pipe, gazing at nothing more
Than a blue-and-white labyrinthine border;

And the waiters wore white shirts and had black hair.
I used to wonder about the name of the place,
The story behind its red italic sign. It sounded

Funny to say, "Meet me in The Chariot today."
One morning I saw a family there with a little boy,
A family lucky enough to get a big booth—

Over by the wall on which appeared
A mural no one ever paid attention to:
It was rendered well but without distinction,

Receding in all that light and noise and bustle;
And there was, after all, no vantage point,
Nowhere to stand and take it in completely,

Unless the whole room emptied out. But their son
Had the perfect angle, because of his size,
Because he wasn't ashamed of being curious.

It was a question he asked that made me see
What was there all along, made me notice
Not only the chariot, with a golden warrior

High in its chair, but lying behind the wheels—
Almost under them—a crumpled wretch of a thing,
Featureless, inert upon the ground. "Who is the winner?"

The boy asked his mother and father. "Who won?"
So I looked up again and saw Hector's body
Being dragged in the dust by Achilles. By the rage

Of Achilles. A horse-drawn chariot, a cartoon corpse,
A clear unchanging sky. In voices difficult to hear,
His parents were explaining the Trojan War.

He didn't care about Helen or Agamemnon, he knew
Someone had lost, someone had won (*Patroclus
Is dead, and now the man who killed the man*

Who killed ... and then ... then ...). "But who
Is the one who won?" he wanted to know:
"Tell me the name of the team. Who won?"

A scraping fork shivered in my ears, echoes
Simmered, thickening the air, as the room contracted
To a scene spinning between the unknowable

And the known. This morning I was sitting
On my bed, finding lines to pull me into the day,
Because I was trying to figure out the path of rage,

How a bed can be a place where it begins
Or where it ends, even a place to figure out
What one is thinking, to grasp what is beyond

Human power. To conceive the need for distance,
Because it is hard to live in one place in one time
With a single mind: the weight of history, or love,

Is too much to bear, too easy to brush aside.
Achilles may be afraid to lose his power,
To relinquish the power he needs to keep

In order to know who he is. I am the same,
Perhaps, but a woman does not fear
Certain things. I could see how Helen

Lost her head, how Achilles lost his,
How Paris was despicable, and yet
Imagining another face, another fate

Was futile. Honor will bury pity, beauty
Burnish slaughter, glory slaughter glory,
A body infuriate fury. But I was getting hungry,

It was time for coffee, time to enter the light, to lose
Myself in the light of the first day of April 2004.
I left the *Iliad* on my bed and opened the door

To get the paper, see the front page: an image
Of bodies—of pieces of bodies—burnt
And suspended. Mangled. Nameless. Beyond

Recognition. Suspended: "on a bridge over
The Euphrates." One of the rivers of Eden.
Distance dissolved, desire and anger

Dissolved, revulsion rising in the face
Of what a piece of clay can become.

THETIS'S LAMENT

Even I, a daughter of the sea,
To whom all waters run,
Even I could not bury
What I knew he would be
When I bore Achilles, my son.

INTERLUDE

Pull out from me this dagger.

> Not a dagger, no.

No, not a dagger. One of the spokes—

> I spoke of the unspoken.

You spoke too soon.

> Too late to say whatever could be said.

In time—

> In time?

The time it takes to speak has been taken.

> I spoke.

A spoke in the wheel of the unspoken.

> You cannot take it back.

That's what it's for, to go on.

> Even if?

Even so.

A peg on which to hang the future.

Something to go on.

Even if it cannot be taken back.

ZENO IN THE DARK

I

Zeno remembers
many things
even when he goes down the hall
in his bedroom slippers

old worn velvet
of a starless night
his one true comfort

if comfort can belong to one for whom
the hall itself is a passage of unmade choices
favorite slippers if one can choose to have
one thing over another

Joy is in the forgetting in the slipping
into something rather than nothing
slipping down the hall

without a light
wondering if he will bump his knee
or break an empty (was it really
empty) glass

II

Zeno like lightning
like honey

like many other things as well
used to think

he was a solitary mountain
a cog

in the machinery of heaven
whose fittings are finer

than a strand a spider spins
to climb up to the sky

III

Even Zeno's name
begins

without dividing

commencing
in a zigzag of delight

parallel horizons

meeting at an angle

Even Zeno's name
ends

without dividing

but Zeno cannot enter
his name

IV

Zeno
sits on a chair
crossing his leg

in the dark
which one which one

doesn't matter
ergo
it matters more

Zeno
sits on a chair

deciding
how to decide
if tomorrow will start

with the left
or the right

V

Then again

if he stubs his toe on the way to bed
if the telephone rings

he will be free to forget
how he got to the end of the hall
he will be free

to consider other things

how he came to the same place
by a different door

how zero can swallow any number
or be at peace
inside another

how a leaf in the wind is a river of color

how the blanket he likes to pull to his chin
was knit by his mother

whose skin is as silky and cracked
as a map he found when he lost himself
in a station in a dream

in a city he has still never seen

ON TIME

Time can be told in the opening of a flower,
Trumpet of dawn, flugelhorn of the sun
Sinking down. Noiseless explosions
Greet an attentive eye. And the ear

Is a flower, too, a welcome home for echoes,
Kisses, and cackles. Cauldron of starlight,
Tincture and blaring cry, whatever brushes
Your senses unlatches a doorway

Scoured by salt, vanishing as you plunder
The coffers of sleep. So you will know
What it means to be utterly free, floating

Without a hope, floating in hope, a medium
Fit for the being you have become, given
The bed you have made, the race you won.

BOY WITH A THORN

Lo Spinario
(bronze, late first century BCE)

A long day, a long run, a long road,
And somewhere on it you felt a pang,
Nothing more. A quiver of lightning,

Nothing to stop for. Only now,
As you sit on the stump of a blasted tree,
Folding one leg over the other,

Drawing it up until your ankle
Strains against your knee, as you study
The sole that is cradled in your hands—

Only now do you notice a small hot rose
Blushing under the skin, where a thorn
Broke into flesh. And you recall

That sudden twinge: a throb subsiding
In a wave, spurring you on past all
Those ochre hills, daring you to keep

A steady pace though you were tired
Of those hills, of pine after twisted pine
Casting a net of needles in your path,

Though a droning in your ears said
The city would fall, that the warning
You carried would never arrive.

Once you were caught in a blinding
Torrent of rain, but the sky stayed blue,
Every other patch of land was dry,

And the air surrounding you sharpened
The horizon, though whatever was in reach
Grew obscure. Later, as you crossed

A familiar field, your fingertips
Stirring the tall grass, your limbs
Remembering a power that seemed to flow

From the overturning chalice of the sun,
A surprising coldness seeped
Through your skin, and a sensation

You did not welcome entered in.
You brushed it aside and it was gone,
And you went on. But it didn't go

Anywhere, it was inside you, blooming...
It is easy to remove the thorn, now
That you can rest, easy to miss the valley

You fled, its flock of shadows grazing
On stone. But sometimes everything
Remains hidden, there is nothing more

Than a scene on an empty amphora,
Nothing new, nothing worth noting,
Until the speed of your body releases

The resin in pine. If this is the first time
You faltered in the middle of everything,
It will not be the last. Today a thorn

Is the cause. Sooner or later,
There will be other things to draw
Out of yourself to recover again

Who you are. It will hurt to pluck it out,
But you will think nothing of it:
See, you are barely wounded.

Later you will long to be that boy
Whose only regret was having to stop
Without wanting to, whose only care

Was a path beaten in the dust
Under his feet: a place where something
Too slight to avoid, too minor

To fear, too random to foresee
Interrupted a journey
Written in the whorls of your skin—

As if your fate, anyone's fate,
Could be written or read.

ALWAYS THE SAME FACE

a few days after the autumn equinox

Full moon. Harvest moon. Late September.
She's trying to get through.

She cannot see us, we cannot see her
Completely. Only one side is ever the side

We see. However it seems, however she appears,
That is always the case, we are told.

And it is so. She cannot get through.
Her light wells, caught in a gray cocoon.

The night before, she shone so clear and far,
All at once entirely free

Of anything that obscures,
Not a cloud in the way, not a single living thing

Flying high, not a tree reaching a great dark arm
Across the bed of the sky, not a ligament

Tying her to any star. But today she is milky,
About to awaken, about to be born entire.

Someone is looking up, someone else is beginning
To say what wanted to be said, someone

Is going to stay, under the blue-black blanket,
Confiding a feeling that seeps into the day.

O blinking eye, lid of the deep, mute
Opaline drum, skin on the surface of sight—

Peel away what may, another side,
Another face unseen

Peers at a nameless where, whose time
Will come. The mother of eternity is there:

Holding a cold mirror, she turns to see
How the solar wind undoes her burning hair.

ALBUM

Why on earth does a postage stamp come to mind
When I see those floating bodies,
Immaculate faces of infants sleeping too deeply
In the wake of the tsunami?

Long ago, a flood overtook the basement,
Almost all the old books in ruins,
Leather bindings buckling, gilded edges fading,
The marbling drifting away.

From the wreckage we pulled the stamp albums
My father kept, and another that was mine,
Holding the countries I longed to visit, lozenges
Of color, names too fragrant to pronounce.

Nations that are no more could slumber there,
Though swallowed or torn;
Mountains, bridges, and flowers survived.
The cover was stained, the pages dried,

But one of the stamps had come undone,
Sliding from corners lovingly fastened—
And now whole shorelines are sliding away,
The book of the world so swollen it cannot close.

BOX IN EDEN

Pink Pearl eraser
rubbing white paper,
diminishing into
a little hill, more

and more so the box
can fill: little container
a perfect promise,
ready to hold the feel

of skin, ready to nestle
a fingernail clipping,
a button, a marble,
a tooth or a pin.

Pink Pearl collecting,
sifted, sifting:
embers of kindness,
a bower of crumbs.

Here resides
whatever in itself
by itself
is enough

to touch, eyes closed,
not to covet or possess,
only to caress—
and where is it now,

my secret compartment,
humble casket,
barrow of being,
storehouse of

unsayable softness
unclaimed, asleep
at the bottom
of what drawer?

NOT A PRAYER

in memoriam CZESŁAW MIŁOSZ

On Lorenzo Lotto's suffering Christ
There are two tears, two drops of blood,
But now that I've heard of your passing

They glimmer differently. Was this
Your gift? For I cannot tell if
The flickering shadow of what is gone

Makes this happen, bare fact suffusing
The skin until our pulse quickens
With the life of another running in

Our own vessels, sending out
Its fluctuating rhythm, a flock of birds
In a net of chance, a shape—of what?

Now that you're on the other side, lifting
An eyebrow at the view, you would know
What to say. Your bridge that is made

Out of prayer, those feet walking over
The river into a cushion of crimson
Anemones... Will you find her there,

That girl on the metro, smiling
An aisle away? Does a waiter turn,
Flashing a silver tray? If only I could fall

Into the arms of my father, asking him
Why he is sad, so that he may weep
The tears he never shed as we marvel

At the symmetry of two drops of water,
Two drops of blood—Lotto's brush
A chrysalis of dust, a butterfly

Who gave herself back to original light
So the worm again can fly. Every mote
Is a spasm of sight, every wound an eye.

ON BETRAYAL

And a voice came to me and said:
People betray each other all the time,
How did you live without knowing this,
What a child you have been, for so long.

Don't you remember how a star started
To flicker then went out in a room dissolving
Into darkness, beside you someone still
Breathing, breathing, wanting to devour

Your body without sharing his soul, wanting
To disown his own spirit, his own ghost
Rising against him, rising against you,

Wrestling a word that may have been the twin
Of silence, a muffled syllable akin to love,
Though if it was it was by hope unfed.

TO THE FOREST

A tree fell on me. There is no other way
to say this. I do not want to explain.
It fell. And I too was a tree, and together

we were thrashing, and it seemed
the sap rose and the rose's thorn—

no, the needles
brushed
against me.

I do not want to say,

I cannot say
this
any other way.

It should be said
only to make it go away.

A tree fell
and rose, and together
we swept the sky.

And one of the other trees said:
I recall someone walking among us,
how she was taken, how it seemed she was
one of us, and then how it seemed
all of us had been like her,

but no, it cannot be,
we are stalwart.

She wanted something to happen
but nothing like that,
she wanted everything but no,
not that,

she didn't want anything at all.

She is many,
as is every
tree
a story of one
and many.

Without a sound it crashed,
burning my skin,
my mouth.

And afterward a rose appeared,
broken but full, and I
carried it home and woke to see it there
and thought it would die but it would not die,

it wanted to be there remembering itself,
mocking the daylight with its blush.

It
be-
fell:

a bell
rang
without sounding,
its tongue
melting
my tongue.

The woodsman said,
the tree must be cut
that did this,

whatever has done this to you
will be split
in two.

·NEWSPAPER MAN

Woke to a figure a man
made of newspaper
a mummified creature
strips of language running
everywhere lines
adding up to nothing

Couldn't find his eyes
but his hands his hands
were everywhere
touching me
with whatever words
whatever empty spaces
made him what he was

Then his eyes too
were everywhere
in every word a pupil
impenetrable

Impossible to tell
what he meant
by being there just
as the glare of morning
hit the window

Woke to a silent figure
whose every pore
sweated ink
who was spreading
the stain of the news
pressing against my skin
marking me with another tattoo

No matter where I looked
there was more to know
more to see
the places I wanted
or never would want to go

But I didn't want
to know his body
to know those things

No matter how polite I was
he wouldn't leave
no matter what I said or did
he wouldn't stop
touching me

Woke to a newspaper man
who lay there all morning
then turned and said to me

Wherever you go a widow
waits in a window
an ark dwells
in the dark

Whatever you do
anguish will be
born in a wish
if you stay if you flee

If you are white as
the flesh of an apple
or black as a seed
at the core

I will be known I will
find you I will bind you
with my body
with my breath

If you let me in if
you keep me at bay
whether you look
or look away

OPEN FIELD

Forget the comma, the crow said, darting
onto another branch, random joy being his,

being mine, being yours, depending on how
you look at a branch, which is, after all,

something essential for him, for you, for me,
his wings no more no less than the wings

of his fellow travelers, his curious, forlorn
pecking at what—a pecking for what is new.

And isn't that what we want, to be taken
out of a sentence into the air, where conversation

blossoms into speechlessness, the bosom
of belonging, being in rather than on, in being here.

But the comma said, how dare you abandon
the curl that tells how distinctly different

one iota is from another, lifting a note a little
higher or lower, casting a shadow over whatever

may follow, or making a sudden clearing
for the future, letting it tremble, hesitate, sing,

announcing how each thing depends on another,
touching, resting, going on, dying and ferreting

too, yes, that too, did you think it impossible to do
another thing after arriving, did you forget the

moment awakening after a dark dry dot,
that jab of ending, a minuscule well sounding

no less no more than a drop of the sap
asleep in winter trees, did you believe for a split

second you could breeze on by or pass
such a point without calling out to its source?

O, said the crow,
but didn't you know:

I
am a drop

of the bottomless well,
you are a mark in the snow.

A RHINOCEROS AT THE PRAGUE ZOO

While ducks and swans paddled placidly on the Vltava's rushing waters, penguins, storks and gorillas were evacuated from the Prague Zoo, and a crane was used to lift two rhinoceros to high ground. But one turned violent and had to be killed, and keepers had to shoot a 35-year-old Indian elephant named Kadir as water rose to his ears and he refused to move to high ground.

The New York Times, August 14, 2002

A blindfolded rhinoceros
is being lifted
out of the water.

It is important he doesn't see
what is going on.

Please pass it on:

please pass along
his blindfold
so we can be lifted, too.

Take us slowly from the flood,
the rising water
that threatens to wash
everything away.

The world keeps unraveling,
the riverbank
dissolving,
the blood flowing,

and the rhinoceros
had better keep
that blindfold on

because he is dangerous
if he sees what is dangerous.

Unlike a unicorn
he is heavy and
clumsy and dumb.

He will crush someone
with his fear,
he will tear us apart
if he panics.

Raise him
gently,
lower him
gently
into a meadow
of cool waters.

Then pass along
the blindfold
so we can be lifted, too.

Raise us
out of the muck
onto a bed of grass,

pass the bright bandana
covering his eyes,
a blanket
of surrender,
a curtain of bliss:

a checkered napkin
taken from a tavern

or a chessboard
seen
from above.

THE OTHER RHINOCEROS

Actually, there were two
It is spelled the same in the singular
Or the plural

Now there is one

What is the plural of flood
Does more water make it plural
No, only more water in more places

A flood
A big flood
A great flood

Water
The water
The waters rising

And no ark
No dove
No branch of an olive

Live
Olive tree
Live

O live
Olive
O live

THE MUSEUM OF STOLEN THINGS

Cairo, January 2001

In Cairo there is a museum
called the Museum of Stolen Things.
It looks more like a house
than a museum: not a forbidding place,
and no one seems to be standing guard.

We were walking in the desert
when we came upon it,
not far from other places filled with tourists.
My friend hadn't noticed it before,
though he has lived in Cairo for many years.

I couldn't bring myself to enter
the Museum of Stolen Things,
and so I cannot tell you what is inside.
I do not know, he does not know,
and his wife, descended from a pharaoh,
does not know, nor their children,
not a single one of them,

though later, when I repeated
the words on its makeshift sign,
all of us were curious to know.

*

By the time we arrived we were all very tired:
we had waited in too many lines, we had seen
too many things,
kings and queens and servants,
tripods of gold, too much gold, too many kingdoms.

By the time we arrived
the Museum of Stolen Things seemed like a joke,
but after a while it became a riddle.

*

The sign itself can be taken
in different ways:
there is nothing inside
because everything has been taken,
or everything inside
is something that has been taken.

Either way, something is missing,
something belonging
to another person, another place, another time.

Either way, everything has been taken.

*

The sign was written by hand, in English,
scrawled in capital letters
at a sharp angle, as if in a hurry.

A figure close by, a man with time
on his hands, was standing at an angle
parallel to the letters of the sign.

There seemed to be all the time in the world.

The sand lay all around us,
unstoppable pouring
of unrecorded infinite moments.

Everything stolen by time was beneath our feet—
maybe that is why it was hard to walk
without wobbling.

A camel kneeled, as it was taught to,
then it rose into the air and swaggered off,
tassels teetering, swaying.

*

I should have insisted on going inside.
After all, I was the visitor, and as a guest
could have had my way.

How could exhaustion overcome curiosity?

*

Perhaps there are many such places
filled with nothing,
only a caption for what is missing,

a placard mounted on a wall saying

here lies,
here is.

Among these grains
someone used to know what lay here,
but this is all there is:

among these grains
here lies.

*

Or could there be an object
severed from its name,
devoid of introduction or conclusion,

its caption moving in the desert
on foot, on four-legged creatures—

a blur in a storm   a streak of light   a banner
without marking or color,

reflecting the sun,

refuting nothing.

CONVERSATION BETWEEN CLOUDS

And one said to the other:
It's different every time, but there was one…

And as they roiled above they seemed to want to be
Something in particular, not just anything,

Becoming, in turn, something altogether other,
Dying out at the edge,

Where the last trace of their former form had been.

And one said to the other:
Think of two creatures lying down, unknowing

They recline upon a substance without body
Floating in the air,

Of the vertigo of knowing this
The moment they arise, a moment carrying the fall

Itself as they fold into each other or fade.

And one said to the other:
Remember, dear, there is nothing below but a sea

Of wind, ribbons of rain, a parachute of snow,
Nothing contains us, but even so

It is wise to hold on to my hand,
Even though

It is a cloud among clouds.

AS LONG AS THERE IS WIND IN THE TREES

They happen to be beside each other, and so they touch
For no apparent reason. Reason enough. They happen

To be beside each other. So they touch. For us
It is not like this, though timorous shadows tell

An arm to move, a head to turn, sensing something
Near, someone who may be one of the ones who,

For no apparent reason, will move away or turn,
Stirring a storm, giving it room to toil, one for whom,

For a time everlasting or brief, you will be the leaf,
The bole, the bee, the light, and the other way around

If you are lucky: if you happen to be in town,
Out of change, by a brook, in the mood, near a shop

Proclaiming a host of spices in a tongue without
An alphabet, a tongue whose sound is the changing

Shade of a cloud, the scent of iron rising after rain,
Curtains of rain opening, pouring down.

KEEP READING

. . . and still, as he looked, he lived; and still,
as he lived, he wondered.
                Kenneth Grahame,
                The Wind in the Willows

"Keep reading," you said, as we lay
In the boat of your bed, you
Almost asleep, I floating on words,

On a stream of lines flowing
To the river's edge, when I stopped,
For I wanted to be by your side,

There with you, your skin warm
Against mine. "Keep reading," you said:
Though I thought you were far away,

On the other side, on the brink of sleep,
You were listening, still, you were near,
Knowing how far from the end I was

As the sound of your voice (as a sound
Alive *inside* your voice) carried me on
To the weir, to a piper piping an alien

Song at the gates of dawn, on a shore
Changed by more than the touch
Of the sun. Then the words wavered,

The letters blurred, swelling
To dapples of darkness and light—
I looked away to see you there,

Your glistening lashes, a tear
That fell, running down your cheek
As you heard me start to weep

At a passage you knew so well,
The one you were longing to hear
As you floated far into night,

Waiting in the boat of your bed
To hear me reach what was so close by,
Where you led me to, having read my heart.

"Keep reading," you said, without saying why.

NOTES

"Born for the Snow": The prophet Isaiah envisions seraphs as celestial beings possessing six wings. Snow crystals take an infinite variety of shapes, but their structure is always hexagonal.

"View from a Terrace in Antibes" is dedicated to the memory of Richard Arthur Wollheim (1923–2003), whose illuminating essay on the life and work of Nicolas de Staël appeared in the *London Review of Books,* July 24, 2003. Born in Saint Petersburg in 1914 and orphaned soon after his aristocratic family fled to Poland during the Russian revolution, de Staël lived much of his adult life in Paris and the south of France. He committed suicide in 1955, jumping from the terrace of his studio in Antibes; the view from that studio is the subject of one of his paintings.

"That Morning": on the night of September 10, 2001, a violent thunderstorm swept through New York, which may account for the exceptional clarity of the sky on the following day.

"The Chariot" refers, in its closing stanzas, to the front-page story of *The New York Times* on April 1, 2004; the article included a photograph of the charred and dismembered remains of four private military contractors from the United States who were killed and mutilated in an ambush on March 31, then hung from the girders of one of Fallujah's bridges. The poem was composed in the early morning, before the newspaper arrived, and then revised.

"Boy with a Thorn" refers to the *Spinario* (thorn-puller), a famous Hellenistic statue of a boy pulling a thorn from the sole of his foot. It was thought to be a portrait of the shepherd Marcius, who, according to legend, died of his wound after warning the people of Rome of an impending attack on their city. The bronze statue is in the collection of the Palazzo dei Conservatori, Capitoline Museums, Rome; copies are in the Uffizi, the British Museum, and the Metropolitan Museum of Art.

"Album" makes reference to the aftermath of the Sumatra-Andaman earthquake of December 26, 2004.

"Not a Prayer" alludes to the "velvet bridge" in Czesław Miłosz's poem "On Prayer."

"The Museum of Stolen Things" is dedicated to Steffen Stelzer. When I visited him and his family in Cairo in January 2001, we went for a walk in the desert, where we happened upon the museum with its makeshift sign. Later we found a listing in the *Lonely Planet* guide to Cairo (1998 edition, edited by Andrew Humphreys), which was evidently published before a sign was posted in English; translating the Arabic sign as "Seized Antiquities Museum," the guidebook describes a building that "houses a random and unconnected assortment of sarcophagi, jewellery, icons, and other antiquities confiscated from would-be smugglers."

"Keep Reading" echoes passages in the final pages of chapter 7, "The Piper at the Gates of Dawn," in *The Wind in the Willows* by Kenneth Grahame.

ACKNOWLEDGMENTS

Grateful acknowledgment is made to the following publications, in whose pages these poems first appeared:

Alaska Quarterly Review, "Not a Prayer" and "The Other Rhinoceros"

The Atlantic Monthly, "Album"

Barrow Street, "Born for the Snow," "My Brother's Shirt," "Zeno in the Dark," "Interlude," and "View from a Terrace in Antibes"

Global City Review, "Newspaper Man" and "To the Forest"

The Kenyon Review, "As Long as There Is Wind in the Trees," "A Needle in the Sky," "Always the Same Face," "Letter to the Snow," and "Open Field"

Literary Imagination, "The Chariot"

The New Republic, "Conversation Between Clouds" and "Inchworm"

The New Yorker, "May Day" and "On Time"

Poetry London, "On Betrayal" and "That Morning"

Poetry Northwest, "Acorn," "A Rhinoceros at the Prague Zoo," and "Tender Offer"

Smartish Pace, "The Museum of Stolen Things"

Washington Square, "Boy with a Thorn"

"Always the Same Face" was also published in *The Inconstant Moon,* a limited letterpress edition with lithographs by Enid Mark (The ELM Press, 2007). "Acorn" also appeared in *Women's Work: Modern Women Poets Writing in English,* edited by Eva Salzman and Amy Wack (Seren Press, 2008). "May Day" was reprinted in the Alhambra *Poetry Calendar 2008,* edited by Shafiq Naz. "Always the Same Face," "Conversation Between Clouds," and "On Betrayal" were featured on *Verse Daily* as the poem of the day.

"A Rhinoceros at the Prague Zoo," "Tender Offer," and "Acorn" received the 2006 Richard Hugo Prize from *Poetry Northwest.*

The author wishes to express her profound gratitude to the John Simon Guggenheim Memorial Foundation for their generous support during the time part of this book was written and to The MacDowell Colony, the Corporation of Yaddo, and the American Academy in Rome for essential residencies. For invaluable criticism, special thanks to Anne Atik Arikha, David Baker, Patricia Carlin, Peter Covino, Amy N. Mack, Elizabeth Macklin, Molly Peacock, Elfie Raymond, and Jack Stacey Shanewise. Thanks to Elena Elenev for her crucial help and to Christie Ann Reynolds, my assistant. Utmost thanks to my editor, Paul Slovak.

ABOUT THE AUTHOR

SHEILA MCKINNON

Phillis Levin is the author of three previous volumes of poetry, *Temples and Fields* (1988), winner of the Poetry Society of America's Norma Farber First Book Award, *The Afterimage* (1995), and *Mercury* (2001), and is the editor of *The Penguin Book of the Sonnet* (2001). She has been a fellow at The MacDowell Colony, Yaddo, and the Liguria Study Center for the Arts and Humanities in Bogliasco, Italy, and is an elector of the American Poets' Corner at the Cathedral Church of Saint John the Divine. Her other honors and awards include an Ingram Merrill grant, a Fulbright Fellowship to Slovenia, the Amy Lowell Poetry Travelling Scholarship, and fellowships from the Guggenheim Foundation and the National Endowment for the Arts. Born in Paterson, New Jersey, and educated at Sarah Lawrence College and the Johns Hopkins University, Phillis Levin has taught at the University of Maryland, the Unterberg Poetry Center of the 92nd Street Y, and in New York University's graduate creative writing program. She is currently a professor of English and poet-in-residence at Hofstra University and lives in New York City.

JOHN ASHBERY
Selected Poems
Self-Portrait in a Convex
Mirror

TED BERRIGAN
The Sonnets

PHILIP BOOTH
Selves

JIM CARROLL
Fear of Dreaming: The
Selected Poems
Living at the Movies
Void of Course

ALISON HAWTHORNE
DEMING
Genius Loci

CARL DENNIS
New and Selected Poems
1974–2004
Practical Gods
Ranking the Wishes
Unknown Friends

DIANE DI PRIMA
Loba

STUART DISCHELL
Backwards Days
Dig Safe

STEPHEN DOBYNS
Mystery, So Long
Pallbearers Envying the One
Who Rides
The Porcupine's Kisses
Velocities: New and Selected
Poems: 1966–1992

EDWARD DORN
Way More West: New and
Selected Poems

ROGER FANNING
Homesick

AMY GERSTLER
Crown of Weeds
Ghost Girl
Medicine
Nerve Storm

EUGENE GLORIA
Drivers at the Short-Time
Motel
Hoodlum Birds

DEBORA GREGER
Desert Fathers, Uranium
Daughters
God
Western Art

TERRANCE HAYES
Hip Logic
Wind in a Box

ROBERT HUNTER
A Box of Rain: Lyrics:
1965–1993
Sentinel and Other Poems

MARY KARR
Viper Rum

JACK KEROUAC
Book of Blues
Book of Haikus
Book of Sketches

JOANNA KLINK
Circadian

ANN LAUTERBACH
Hum
If in Time: Selected Poems,
1975–2000
On a Stair

CORINNE LEE
PYX

PHILLIS LEVIN
May Day
Mercury

WILLIAM LOGAN
Macbeth in Venice
Night Battle
Vain Empires
The Whispering Gallery

MICHAEL MCCLURE
Huge Dreams: San Francisco
and Beat Poems

DAVID MELTZER
David's Copy: The Selected
Poems of David Meltzer

CAROL MUSKE
An Octave Above Thunder
Red Trousseau

ALICE NOTLEY
Disobedience
In the Pines
Mysteries of Small Houses

LAWRENCE RAAB
The Probable World
Visible Signs: New and
Selected Poems

BARBARA RAS
One Hidden Stuff

PATTIANN ROGERS
Generations

WILLIAM STOBB
Nervous Systems

STEPHANIE
STRICKLAND
V: WaveSon.nets/Losing
L'una

TRYFON TOLIDES
An Almost Pure Empty
Walking

ANNE WALDMAN
Kill or Cure
Marriage: A Sentence
Structure of the World
Compared to a Bubble

JAMES WELCH
Riding the Earthboy 40

PHILIP WHALEN
Overtime: Selected Poems

ROBERT WRIGLEY
Earthly Meditations: New
and Selected Poems
Lives of the Animals
Reign of Snakes

MARK YAKICH
Unrelated Individuals Forming
a Group Waiting to Cross

JOHN YAU
Borrowed Love Poems
Paradiso Diaspora